INSIGHTS TOWARD INTERDEPENDENCE

SCARS TO STARS

EVOLVING MYSTICAL HUMANIST UU
A MEMOIR OF HEAD, HEART, AND SOUL

INDEPENDENCE

OUR
COMMON
GOOD

INTERDEPENDENCE

DOLLY HAIK-ADAMS BERTHELOT

Energion Publications
Gonzalez, Florida
2021

ISBN13: 978-1-63199-793-8
eISBN: 978-1-63199-794-5

Energion Publications
P. O. Box 841
Gonzalez, Florida 32560

energion.com

ABOUT SCARS TO STARS

How did a devout Catholic girl from a Louisiana mill town become a Mystical Humanist Unitarian Universalist, and what does that mean anyway, at least to her?

"Dr. Dolly" shares her emotional journey—torn from Catholicism by a young love crisis, jumping from daily news editor to innovative existential journalism teacher, world traveling writer-photographer, professor, communication consultant, later medical and caretaking challenges, and loss. Life spurred endless questions plus visions of possible ongoing evolution.

What matters, she says, isn't theories, religion, or even God. Not beliefs but behaviors. Whether it's practiced or not, the Golden Rule is preached across every religion and is at the solid core of Humanism. Never has there been a greater need for interdependence and commitment to Our Common Good. The COVID-19 pandemic, racial and political turmoil, climate upheaval—all have shown we must cooperate to flourish or we may perish.

Speaking from both head and heart, the author rejects the dualism that too often separates interlocking reality. While embracing the logic of humanism and principles of Unitarian Universalism, she also shares key stories and poems revealing mystical experiences and the potency of dreams.

This brief ethical and spiritual memoir is compelling, edifying, and inspiring, with a touch of wit. It celebrates beauty and art (such as that in her cover photograph), honesty, authentic relationships, intellect and intuition, critical and creative thinking, freedom and responsibility, unity within diversity, and the open-mindedness that lets in sunbeams and fresh air.

1 PHILOSOPHICAL OVERVIEW

Two childhood buddies, now middle aged, are strolling together in a park. The preacher is concerned about the soul of his old friend, who has long been an atheist, so he often pushes his position. "But what if everyone gave up God? We'd have only lying, cheating, stealing, raping, murders..."

The atheist replies, "Hmm, we certainly have too much of all that now, and often done by 'believers.' But tell me, my friend, if you gave up God, is that what you would do?"

Without God or traditional religious beliefs of some kind, is that what you would do? Can you be a good person? Lead a rich, fulfilling life? Rear a good kid? Cope with illness, loss, and death?

My life experience suggests yes. This book does not provide a scholarly approach nor attempt to answer for everyone; it is merely a short overview of one person's story of personal growth and the perspective that has grown from that experience.

I am not, in fact, a proclaimed atheist, yet I do live without a god and without a traditional religious creed or practice. God doesn't matter to me, people do. All people.

Mystical Humanist. Some purists might consider these terms antithetical. They seem at least paradoxical. So what? I am, as it happens, quite comfortable with paradox. And with

1

ambiguity. I have always resonated with Ralph Waldo Emerson's contention, "A foolish consistency is the hobgoblin of little minds." Fortunately, my current Unitarian Universalism is broad and open enough to embrace all of who I am —and presumably all I may yet become.

I have no idea whether there is or isn't some being or entity that some may call God. I choose to avoid the term (except sometimes in deeply rooted exclamations." Oh, God, oh god!," Occasionally I still call the name in pleas I consider irrational but may use anyway. "Please God! Sweet Jesus...). Nothing in the way I try to live my life would change, one way or the other, whether there is or is not any sort of afterlife, god image, Creator God or whatever. And I chose that word "whatever" not casually but purposely. I certainly don't know whether death is the end of all. But here are a few perspectives I tend to hold at this moment, long after the college student who left Catholicism and the feisty young teacher who embraced Existentialism.

1. Any meaningful deity is likely to be so far beyond our ken that he she it they is/are nothing like most humans envision. The fleas on a dog or cat don't understand or grasp the animal that nourishes them. Surely they could not fathom its essence. Perhaps humans and "higher powers" are similarly related.
2. Any deity worth much would not, I imagine, favor those who behave well or do good in order to meet him her it them and enjoy a blissful eternity. Isn't behaving for the Common Good its own reward? Isn't trying to behave for the well-being of others and the world a higher level of morality than doing so for those future jelly beans? I decided that long before encountering Kohlberg's stages

2

of moral reasoning indicating something similar, but it was nice to know he agreed with me. He has theological credentials I don't. I merely have some humanalogical inclinations.

3. I strive to behave in ways that are positive for humans, and secondarily for other creatures, and the earth and the cosmos. My focus is clearly human beings living in this life. That's quite enough of a challenge. Figuring out what some god wants or demands seems to be foolhardy and unproductive. Any rational god will want rational decision-making. Any compassionate god will want compassionate decision-making. Any god I would want would be both rational and compassionate, like the humans I try to emulate. I fall short of my ideals, like every other mortal, but I try, like most of us.

4. Though I'm not an atheist, I often behave like one, for example, in avoiding the word God and other traditional religious language. Some proclaimed atheists tend to be rather absolutist, seeming as sure there is no god as many fundamentalist Christians are sure of all Biblical meaning. And both can seem as arrogant, in my humble opinion, as anyone cock sure of anything. Absolutist atheists may be as eager as religious proselytizers to influence others in their direction. That is a very natural human inclination. As a writer and teacher I also try to influence people—toward what I consider rational and compassionate behavior—but I have no inclination to belittle religious faith or dissuade the traditionally religious from their faith, if it seems to be sustaining, consoling, or otherwise benefitting them (as it often does seem to)—and if it does not cause direct harm to

them or to others. I gratefully welcome all sincere prayers and blessings as I would any good wishes.

5. I also wouldn't call myself agnostic, for that also defines in terms of a deity, simply expressing a lack of certitude one way or another. God is irrelevant to me. Though the concept of a deity can be intriguing to ponder, it does not impact my ethical beliefs and my behavior. And behavior is far more consequential than belief.

6. At 77, I'm sure of much less than I was at 17 or at 27. Uncertain of anything theological and post mortem, I do gladly embrace these ideals: beauty, truth/honesty/trustworthiness, critical *and* creative thinking, intellect *and* intuition, life *and* fictional stories, gratitude, empathy, kindness, love, independence *and* interdependence, unity *within* diversity, Our Common Good, freedom *and* responsibility, and possibility, perhaps infinite possibilities. I try to avoid overgeneralization and dualistic thinking and to consider nuances and "both-and."

7. Although "spirit" may be undefinable and immeasurable, it is vital. The spirit we feel, embrace, and project is more important than our professed beliefs. And how we behave toward others matters most of all. I know people of great and generous spirit who represent many faiths and none at all.

2

RELIGIOUS AND PERSONAL ROOTS

How did a devout Roman Catholic mid-20th Century small-town Southern girl become a Mystical Humanist UU, and what does all that mean anyway? At least what does it mean to me? My husband, Dr. Ron Berthelot, who was naturally a man of few words and not really a wordsmith, surprised me when he (not I) coined the paradoxical combo "Mystical Humanist" to describe himself, and I immediately knew it was perfect for me as well. For all our differences (and there were many), we had tended to be in philosophical sync since our first evening together, in June 1966. We'd spent hours just talking about such matters, including, of all things for a first date of sorts, the Ten Commandments and how most of them made reasonable sense for people to live in society. He had also left Catholicism, just as emphatically as I, but with much less soul searching, trauma, and drama. Catholicism had never meant as much to him as to me. By that time, however, we had arrived at essentially the same place. From there, over most of our 45 years together, we continued similar philosophical growth, into Mystical Humanist Unitarian Universalists.

Most of my first two decades were spent in Bogalusa, Louisana, a now sadly deteriorating town associated primarily with the stench of the paper mill that sits right in the original business center. Yet I increasingly cherish my roots. I was the first of what became seven children of two hard-working first-generation Americans.

Mama's parents were both from Lebanon, Eastern Orthodox Christians who became and remained Roman Catholic, wed in 1903 New Orleans, owned dry good stores, and, during the Depression, moved to Bogalusa (within spitting distance of Mississippi). Mom was the youngest of eight children of Espir Saba Haik and Tamam O'Feish Haik.

Dad's parents were Jesse Fielding Adams and Clara Giorgi Adams. His Mother was a War Bride who came from Germany pregnant with my future Dad. Grandma Adams wound up raising two sons without the lame, troubled alcoholic World War I Veteran who left them. She and her boys were also Catholic.

SUPER CATHOLIC FAMILY

Once that young Lebanese-German/mixed American couple married and had me and eventually six others, we all went to Annunciation Catholic Church and School. We were a distinct minority in a mostly "hard-shelled Southern Baptist" town. I was chosen to play Mary at least twice, briefly contemplated becoming a nun, wrote and directed a little drama about St. Polycarp (all I recall now is he was a martyr). In my beloved class of 17, I earned the gold religion pin at 8th Grade graduation, where I cried inconsolably over leaving that sheltered little world.

At the big bad Bogalusa Junior High and High School, I was often asked to answer questions about our strange-to-many religion that so differed from the local norm. I prided myself on knowing "the answers" and being able to explain understandably. My Dad led the Knights of Columbus. Mom's eldest sister, my Aunt Laurice Haik Zoghby, had married Herbert Zoghby of Mobile and they had seven children before he drowned in the nearby Gulf of Mexico (my first exposure to death at age four). Two of Aunt Laurice's seven children grew up to become priests, two became nuns. Get it? We were as Catholic as it gets.

3

TRANSFORMATIVE TRAUMA

The following story remains, with the exception of marriage and motherhood, the single most pivotal event of my life. It will explain how I catapulted away from that strict and very solid grounding toward the questions that prompted my ongoing life evolution.

I was a 19-year-old sophomore at Southeastern Louisiana College (now Southeastern Louisiana University) in Hammond. "Brian" and I had been going together over a year, were madly in love, and planned to marry.

I remember a clear image of his chubby face and killer smile and I hold sweet recollections of heavenly dancing to "Moon River," a still lovely song that never fails to touch me. Brian graduated from Bogalusa High the year before me and (as far as I know) didn't go to college.

I'm not sure what he did after high school, or even what he intended to do with his life. He was an attractive, charming, popular guy with, I would now surmise, absolutely no depth whatsoever. I'd guess he became a salesman, a good one.

Religion was the stumbling block for Brian and me. My being a devout Catholic and product of a strict Catholic family conflicted with Brian's Pentecostalism. Although he wasn't even practicing, he was too committed to his family's faith—or to his own ego, who knows?—to agree to rear our children Catholic, as was then rather unfairly required.

I had remained a virgin, in spite of our passion, and he "respected me" too much to push for sex. I took to heart the folksy admonishment of my best friend's mother who often drawled: "Keep your legs crossed and your mind on Jesus." I tried my damndest to stay pure as the priest and my parents preached—and work out this niggling denominational dilemma.

A WINDOW OF QUESTIONING OPENED

The conflict opened a window of questioning in my mind that would never close. How could it be right for two people in love to be blocked by their faith? How could one religion require that a person promise his children to another? How could two religions both be "the one true way"?

While I wrestled with weighty religious issues, Brian, I was to learn, was tumbling more physically with "Helen," one of the infamous town sluts, as we then unkindly judged.

My first hint came during what was merely a fun romp through the French Quarter with two friends. Kathy, my best friend since 5th grade, and Barbara, a quirky arty SLU friend and roommate from New Orleans. On a lark, we happened into a Fortune Teller shop, expecting nothing more than to share some silliness. All good Catholics, we certainly didn't believe in such things, but we were curious. We each went in separately for our private readings—and ultimately left together completely shocked.

That woman, with no woo woo fanfare and only a glass of water on the table, told each of us very precise, very specific things that made perfect sense in relation to our very different circumstances.

As for the future, among other things, the seer said to me, "I see a wedding," which delighted me. And then, "And a severance." That news was both puzzling and distressing. This strange stranger's veracity put a crack in what I thought I knew about the world.

That prescient Fortune Teller, and my Mother, and the Ouija Board all had insights I then lacked. Unknown to me, Mama had heard rumors about Brian and Helen, and, like a mother lioness protecting her nearly grown babe, had called them into the back of our family's Adams Red and White Grocery store to ferret out the truth! Small towns and close families afford such checks and balances, but they aren't foolproof. Brian and Helen denied any involvement.

DISTRESSING OUIJA MESSAGE

Around that same period, on one of the few times friends and I used a Ouija Board in my dorm room, it spelled out words that essentially revealed what was to happen—or what had happened, unknown to me. Asked "Will I marry Brian?" the magic triangle raced to the word "No!" And to my shocked "Why not?" spelled "baby" and "alcohol." Still a skeptic of the occult or psychic at that time, I tried to dismiss the message. However, my own mind knew more than I admitted. Just before the Ouija revelation, I wrote haiku poems about misguided trust. My words surprised me, as they often do. I wish I had kept that intuitive poetry.

Trust and honesty have always been among my deepest values, my most cherished ethics. As a child, I recall lying to my mother only once, on some trivial matter, and the burden was so great that I confessed two years later. The fib had been so inconsequential that Mom shrugged it off. She had no idea what I was talking about.

Once, when my parents found a cut in the vinyl seat of our 50's kitchen chair, they questioned my younger sisters, Carolyn and Rita, and me. I was shocked and appalled that they would have doubted me for a moment. If I had done it, denial would not have been an option! Even as a "rebellious teenager," I chose to argue for my rights and wishes, rather than (like my more pragmatic younger siblings) smiling and nodding deceptively and doing as I pleased.

As a super trustworthy person, I expected such virtue in others, and was, therefore, super trusting, thus super vulnerable to betrayal.

HOPE AND BETRAYAL

After Brian and I had a period of strain and a brief break up to contemplate the religious quandary, things were getting better and better and more hopeful between us. My tight window of religious sureness was opening to the fresh air of open-mindedness. One day at Mass I'd experienced a quiet reassurance, almost an audible voice telling me "don't panic," indicating that I had time to resolve my religious and romantic conflict. I truly did relax a bit, after that.

A moment in the college library helped me move forward. I don't remember looking for anything related to the religious questions that were tormenting me, yet an ideal book seemed to find its way into my hands. I now believe it was Huston Smith's *The World's Religions*, which would become a classic. Inside the cover, I saw a list of quotes from various religions—but they were, I saw, virtually the same edict in different words: the Golden Rule, the essence of that which I held dear: Treat people right, as you would want to be treated. So maybe, I thought for the first time, specific religions are not the point!

Thereafter, discussion of marriage became more frequent and more fathomable.

WEDDING RINGS AND REVELATIONS

The night my world toppled made no sense whatsoever. That fateful Friday evening Brian and I actually window shopped for wedding rings. Why did he do that? I will always wonder.

Near the stroke of curfew (was it 11 p.m. in those more innocent times?) Brian walked me up the tall dormitory steps as usual and dropped the bombshell that would change my life: He had been seeing Helen—though of course she "meant nothing" to him. At Mardi Gras, while he was drunk, they had had sex. He'd recently learned that she was pregnant with his child. And, being a "good guy," he felt he should marry her—although he loved me and always would.

In a state of shock, I stammered, "Uh huh. I'm sorry," and walked zombie-like into the dorm.

Messages from my mother were piled on a metal spindle at the check-in desk. The communal hallway phone was ringing for me as I walked in. Mother. I stood and listened while she (believing that I now knew everything) expressed loving concern and anger over the duplicity she had witnessed first hand: "How could they sit right there lying to me when she was pregnant and them already married!" She assumed I knew.

I simply fainted. Blacked out on the old black vinyl tile floor. Somehow, it was even worse knowing that not only the sex, and the baby, but the marriage itself was a done deal. And he was still lying to me! It was like waking from minor surgery to find all limbs amputated. Without consent. Unthinkable!

MOVING FORWARD

The next day, Mother with my second sister, Rita, six years younger than me, drove down (about an hour from Bogalusa) to make sure I was all right. Amazingly, I was. I remember us all sitting on the single beds talking, the only time any of my busy family ever came into my college world. Somehow, I felt remarkably strong, fortified by a solid core of self-confidence, righteous indignation, and loving support.

That night, after a few tears and hours of talking, friends and I had a ritual burning (long before I had ever heard of such practices), igniting Brian's letters in my dorm room's metal trash can. That was stupid, dangerous, I realized as the blaze flared, but also cleansing. We doused the fire as it started to get out of bounds. And we laughed a lot.

I resolved not to let this whole mess damage or embitter me, but to learn from it. I knew I would survive, and be all the stronger for this loss. I saw that neither a religion nor a person should dominate your life, that I had to make my own path, create a life beyond any man. And I would do so. Till then college life had been filled with classes and Brian; there was little time—or inclination—for my own development.

Within a week I got involved in theater, which I had loved in high school and have since, and I resumed my prior newspaper work by creating a freewheeling column, "Thinking On," in the weekly *Lion's Roar*. That column became so popular and respected that it earned me the editor's role the next year; that helped pay expenses and spurred my early journalism career which has impacted everything since.

In fiction, the Brian story might end here. But life is not completely logical, and progress is rarely a straight path. Some months later, susceptible to Brian's earnest pleas, I almost slipped back into his arms. When he insisted he intended to divorce Helen as soon as the baby was born (such gallantry) and begged me for reconciliation, I am embarrassed to admit, I reconsidered, briefly.

Fortunately, my own growth, my parents' horrified reaction, and Brian's repeat performance saved me. Betrayal doesn't always kill love, at least not instantly. I wanted to be with him. My parents went berserk (I could not tell a lie, remember) and insisted that I never see him again. The evening of that parental confrontation, I ran over to the little park behind our house, lay on the ground, cried, and prayed. God was still a friend to depend on then. Admittedly, I sometimes miss him.

Shortly thereafter, I saw Brian only once, a clandestine meeting at the home of a college friend in New Orleans. I told him I would not see him until the divorce was final, a year or so later. (Fortunately, Louisiana required this waiting period.) We both professed undying love. Yeah, right.

Some months later, while I was dating a new and much better man whose proposal I refused, I heard the rumor that Brian was seeing a redhead in Baton Rouge. They soon married. I never heard from him again, and barely cared.

LONG TERM IMPACTS

Through the years Mom passed on sad stories of Brian's son, a fatherless child, who grew, rather predictably, into a petty criminal. I have always felt some responsibility for this boy's fate, the child who almost seemed half mine. For years, on trips home to Bogalusa, I sometimes automatically glanced about, for a boy, and then a man who resembled my misguided love. I've even managed some sympathy for the boy's mother, who no doubt had her own demons and suffering.

"Brian Wiggins" transformed a naive small town Catholic virgin with no real goals beyond marriage into a determined academic, a professional woman, a feminist, eventually an Existentialist/Humanist/Mystical Unitarian Universalist. A girl who probably wouldn't have made it through a B.A. degree at the almost local college, became a world-travelled writer, a teacher, professor, and doctoral level communication specialist, married 45 years to a man far superior to Brian Wiggins, and the mother of a cherished son quite unlike Brian Junior. It could easily have been otherwise.

If only we all knew the benefits our trials and tragedies could bring, perhaps we could face them more gladly. Victor Hugo wrote, "What makes night within us may leave stars." I like that. From scars to stars.

Too bad I never saw Brian again. I never had a chance to stun him with one important message: "Thank you, Brian. Thank you so much!"

4 UNCHURCHED EXISTENTIAL EXPLORERS

For two decades after the Brian fiasco, I gave up not only Catholicism, but god and all organized religion. I didn't consider setting foot in any church, temple, or synagogue except for rare weddings, christenings, confirmations, funerals, or celebrations of life, milestones important to people who were important to me. I felt absolutely no lack, no yearning for something else, and assumed I never would.

Life was full and rich with a marriage, a series of interesting, creative, and fulfilling professional experiences—daily news and feature journalist then editor in Hammond, teacher in East Tennessee, freelance magazine writer and photographer living in Turkey and Germany with extensive travel as a travel writer and photographer, one year mostly covering the circus in Sarasota, return to East Tennessee for grad school and creation of the 1976 U. S. Bicentennial publication for that area, a masters and ultimately doctorate at the University of Tennessee in Knoxville, move to Pensacola for an "assured" academic position that never materialized, an unexpected pregnancy and the exuberance of early Motherhood, double life living in New Orleans, serving on the Loyola University Communication Faculty while Ron kept our beloved young son in our cherished antique Bayou Bungalow and we all spent weekends, holidays, and summers together.

PASSIONATE TEACHER-LEARNER

But let's review that period. Although ethics always mattered greatly to me, after that painful departure from Catholicism at about 20, I was glad to be free, and felt no need to re-enter any religious world in any form. No Thank You!

And for 20 years, I did not. My focus was my marriage to a Louisiana Cajun and to my early meandering careers.

Eager to get out of Louisiana and explore the great beyond, Ron and I first made it to the mountains of East Tennessee. I gave up the daily newspaper life I loved in Hammond for the unknown in Oak Ridge, briefly tried then left a good-paying contract editing gig at the Atomic Energy Commission for a more gratifying experience in education: completing the year teaching English to lovable 7th and 8th graders in an Appalachian coal-mining town so impoverished I still smell the toothache meds we put on student's cavities in lieu of dentists they couldn't afford. Had it not required a commute through mountains, I might have stayed.

Then I relished three exciting though controversial years at Oak Ridge High School. ORHS was innovative enough to allow me to follow my creative spirit in several very natural directions. I was hired to teach journalism, creative writing, and English lit, and to advise the student newspaper, *The Oak Leaf*. That then typical monthly publication was quickly transformed into a dynamic weekly that grappled with some serious issues of the late 1960s early '70s, including abortion, freedom and responsibility, and societal fragmentation, plus school news and conflicts. The transformed weekly was controversial, of course, and soon won highest possible awards, including the prestigious International Gallup Award. I also advised the literary magazine, the *Equinox*.

Students and I worked deep into evenings, many of us forming close relationships that continue to this day. Those students were outstanding—smart, often brilliant, creative, dedicated. Unlike some teachers, I was not at all intimidated by having students who may have had higher IQ and certainly had a stronger socio-economic and intellectual home background than I did.

We weren't in competition, after all, but in cooperation. In contrast to my high school graduate mill worker/small store owner parentage, many were the children of world-class scientists who had been involved with developing the bomb or subsequent scientific research. Scientists like I had worked with at the AEC. My students would go to top-tier colleges and universities that I could never have considered or afforded. Yet we were an ideal match at the perfect time.

And still, with the fervor of young adulthood, I wanted more. In addition to the long hours I already worked, I enthusiastically added to the special new optional courses curriculum and grabbed the opportunity to initiate, develop and teach other topics that were becoming dear to my heart.

BLACK VOICES

Black Voices was perhaps a strange thing for a white girl from a racially problematic little Southeast Louisiana mill town to initiate and take on, but I was eager to do so. I came to appreciate works by James Baldwin, Ralph Ellison, Richard Wright, Langston Hughes, Paul Lawrence Dunbar, and Gwendolyn Brooks as much as any I'd read in American or English literature. My schools had included no African American authors. Until ORHS and UT, except for one sociology major at SLC, all my schools had been segregated.

I was excited to design and implement my unique version of race relations and black lit, incorporating and adapting concepts from a group dynamics course I loved and also an independent studies course, both in Ed Psych at the University of Tennessee in nearby Knoxville.

Humanistic psychology, Carl Rogers *et al*, so enthralled me that I named our beloved spitz dog Esalen, after Esalen Institute, a leading Big Sur California Coast Center for exploring human potential. Nurturing human potential was my teaching goal, stimulating and facilitating critical and creative thinking, whatever the subject matter. Having never even previously seen a book by a black author, I eagerly devoured them for my own education along with my students'.

My classroom was a place for rousing open discussions and some more physical humanistic psychology type activities such as forming and breaching human circles to practice the experience of exclusion and inclusion. (This was the underpinnings of my much later communication consulting explorations and seminars into various ethnicities and cultures and the use of innovative activities, dialogue and personal stories to connect people across all kinds of differences, to teach adults Unity in Diversity, and conflict management.)

While such Black Studies was rare if not unique in late 1960s-early '70s public schools, teaching Existentialist Lit was even weirder. I was practicing existentialism before I ever read about it or knew the term. The Oxford English Dictionary defines existentialism as a philosophical theory or approach that emphasizes the existence of the individual persona as a free and responsible agent determining one's own development through acts of the will. I was attracted to and drew from novels by Jean-Paul Sartre, Albert Camus, Fyodor Dostoevsky, and Franz Kafka. The philosopher Søren Kierkegaard, reflected my belief that each individual—not society or religion—is solely responsible for giving meaning to life and living it passionately and authentically.

At that time I also embraced the existential concept of nothingness, assuming death was the end of everything for an individual's existence. Unlike many, I did not consider this a "philosophy of despair" but rather an incentive to live and embrace this life fully, sure that it is all we have. The concept of self direction rather than other direction drew me in. In psychological terms, I had long had a natural internal rather than external locus of control, so existentialism fit my strong sense of individualism. I was then more sure of many things than I would be after the rough education of experience.

Decades later, I still value much in existential perspective, but I have experienced, not only wider and deeper intellectual exposure, but enough strains, shocks, and sadness to no longer feel in total control of my destiny. Age is certainly humbling.

MULTICULTURAL ADVENTURERS

Being the breadwinner then while Ron was a grad student might have tempered my brazenness; it didn't. I pushed boundaries a bit beyond tolerance, and my contract was not renewed at the end of my third year, when tenure would have been required. Losing that beloved teaching job before getting tenure hurt, but the student, parent, and wider community uproar, Human Relations Commission support, and expressed ACLU interest were all gratifying. Had I stayed to fight the decision, the case may have become a milestone for student press freedom.

However, Ron and I still yearned to explore the world. The ORHS loss led to that opportunity and the most exciting period of my life: two years living, working, and traveling abroad. Again, a negative brought positives. More scars to stars.

Ron spotted an ad at UT for a position with U. of Maryland Extension on military bases in Europe. We grabbed it, quickly sold our home, two cars, and nearly all possessions, and within a month were thrilled to be plopped in Karamursel, Turkey, a two-hour "dolmush" and ferry ride to Istanbul.

I had long felt I was born with the urge to see the world strapped to my soul. My spirit soared during that intense period of exploring foreign climes, interacting with locals across Turkey and much of Western and Eastern Europe, and an unforgettable jaunt to Ethiopia.

We thrived, learning and growing every minute. One published article led to a flow of others and we both further developed the photography skills we had shared since Hammond. That erratic income stream plus Ron's steady paycheck and our low cost of living on military bases paid for our constant travels over always long weekends and 10-day term breaks.

Had a family crisis at home not altered our plans, we would likely have stayed another year or more, but we had packed decades of living and learning into that short period.

Feeding my enthusiasm for multi-cultural explorations and gaining magazine writing and photography experience fortified me to do more of all that in this country. After a year of Ron teaching in Sarasota and me falling in love with the circus (another subculture to write about, not join) we returned to Knoxville for UT grad school. *Pioneer Spirit 76,* the US Bicentennial Anthology I created against all odds focused on the Smoky Mountains area, its people, history, and nature—a culture as different and as intriguing to me as the Moslems in Turkey.

5

SNOWY HOOKY SURPRISE!

So, how did I shift from impassioned career woman grad student to obsessed Mother? Unexpectedly.

I was deeply engrossed in my doctoral program at UT when an historic snowstorm changed everything. Ron and I were leading one of our several double lives for professional purposes. Since beginning his fall 1976 position at Pensacola Junior College (now Pensacola State College), he was renting on Pensacola Beach with two new friends while I kept our Knoxville home, sharing it with a friend and former student to finish my coursework toward a doctorate combining Communication/Journalism emphasis and Educational Curriculum and Instruction/Higher and Adult Education emphasis.

Ron and I had just flown back to Pensacola from a terrific five-day post-Christmas trip to Mexico City and I would normally then have flown back to Knoxville for the early 1977 term. But Knoxville's extreme winter weather made it easy for me to tarry until the next week, luxuriating in hooky time with my husband.

The second we made love that beautiful afternoon, I knew I was pregnant. I was terrified. This was NOT in the plans! After a decade on the pill, for health reasons I'd gone off it for those mostly separated months, and we were generally careful to avoid unprotected sex during danger times. Till then. The impromptu failure for me to leave as planned simply distracted us from such matters. We ran upstairs to the beachfront apartment's only phone and frantically called the Women's Center. They verified my fears: Yes, I was likely ovulating, and no, there was no "after pill."

Now, Ron and I had not decided never to have a child; we had both simply been—and were certainly then—education and career-focused. I was 32; Ron, 38.

Weeks later I was alone with the UT doctor getting verification.

The doctor said rotely, "Congratulations, you are pregnant." I burst into tears.

"What's wrong?" He practically sneered. "You are married, aren't you?"

As a feminist with strong professional aspirations, I was furious that in 1977 this man could think of no other reason for a woman to feel negative about an unplanned pregnancy.

Being separated by 500 miles, Ron and I could discuss this only by phone, at long distance rates, until the weekend I would fly back (yes, this double life was costly). We agreed only to consider all options.

DREAM GUIDANCE

The most important decision of my life came to me in a dream. Vividly. Unequivocally.

In the dream I was bulbously pregnant, sitting on a toilet. Suddenly the baby fell out into the bowl, apparently a miscarriage. I cried and cried, "I want my baby, I want my baby." I woke whimpering those words and knew it was absolutely true. I wanted my baby! Even now, 44 years later, I tear up in the telling, feeling a flood of gratitude for that dream. Without it, I'm not sure what would have happened, but any choice may have lacked the certitude of that message so powerfully presented by my deepest subconscious.

I was then and remain a respecter of dreams. Years later another dream gave me *PERFECTLY SQUARE*, a little book that I still consider my most important writing, and other dreams have provided other significant insights. But no dream meant more than that one, so clearly insisting on Motherhood.

Fortunately, that weekend, as Ron and I walked the then solitary beach and discussed realities, he too was inclined in the birth direction, and we never wavered. We soon loved our forming baby passionately; 3 months into pregnancy, we had named Destin (or Destin Elaine if a girl) a nod both to the fate that seemed so right and the nearby town that had first drawn us to this Northwest Florida Gulf Coast, allowing all the rest to happen.

MYSTICAL COMMON MIRACLE

After a difficult yet glorious natural birth and terrifying seconds with the cord around our baby's neck, childbirth brought the single most cosmic, most euphoric, most mystical moment of my life. I felt at one with everything and everyone, particularly with every woman across time and space who had also known this incredible moment of creating a human being. And the love was unequaled, unknowable to anyone who hasn't experienced parenthood.

However "inconvenient" to my intended path, the first few years were blissful. I was in my last few classes, nearly all but dissertation when I got pregnant. Oops, recalculate, readjust. I quickly completed coursework and rejoined Ron in Pensacola, where we bought and improved our antique

Bayou Bungalow. My reading shifted to books on pregnancy, childbirth, child development, and parenting.

After nearly a two year hiatus from all things grad school (except for continuing payments!), I returned to that work, from our Pensacola home. My beloved toddler saw me researching and writing so often that one of his first sentences was "You working on your dissertation, Mommy?"

6

BECOMING UNITARIAN UNIVERSALISTS

A few years later, having a child nudged me back to organized religion, but certainly not to my parents' religion, or anything remotely similar.

The first religious related quandary came when my dear Uncle Saba Haik died suddenly in New Orleans, while serenely watching television. After Uncle Saba's memorial service, my pre-schooler asked, "Where did he go, Mommy?" And I had no idea what to say.

It was admittedly tempting to use the platitudes with which I'd been raised, the nice, consoling concept of "Uncle Saba is in heaven, darling, with his parents, my Sittie and Papa, and his brother, my Uncle Louis. And with God and all the Angels." That would have been so easy. Yet it would have been disingenuous, and I believed fiercely in truth and authenticity, no matter my child's age.

But what was true? How the hell should I know? I hadn't died, and I knew no one who had died and returned to present the facts. He's in the ground being eaten by worms or was burned up into ashes didn't seem quite suitable for my darling 3-year-old.

I snuggled our son and uttered the only thing I could honestly say "Well, honey, no one really knows what happens to people when they die. People have many different ideas. Some think they go to a better place they call heaven. All I know is the love we have for them goes on as long as we live, so in our memories and hearts, they stay with us."

Although that seemed to satisfy my child, right then I wished I had the benefit of others who might share my perspective and help me navigate through life's big questions without falling back on the easiest alternative, the programming of my own youth, or something similar.

A *VERY* DIFFERENT KIND OF RELIGION

Like many, especially then in the Deep South, I had not even heard of Unitarians or Unitarian Universalists until three exposures in the late 1960s, all in Oak Ridge. One of my favorite plays of that era, Jules Feiffer's "Little Murders" included an hysterical wedding scene with an offbeat humanist Unitarian Minister. Secondly, I was maid of honor in a dear friend's simple wedding in an actual Unitarian Fellowship Hall. Margaret had nabbed her gown for $3 in a bargain basement sale, and looked lovely. Her sister and I wore long tie die skirts. Those were the days, my friend. The couple were Jewish/atheist and former Episcopal.

Third, and perhaps most important, several of my outstanding Oak Ridge High School students had been Unitarians. I filed away this awareness, thinking that if I ever wanted any kind of spiritual sustenance or a free-thinking religious community, I might check out Unitarians. In 1969, Unitarians incorporated the smaller Universalist denomination to become that mouthful that is more easily called UU.

A decade later, in Pensacola, an old college friend, an academic scientist-poet combo, was also UU, and she thought I might be. I noticed in the local daily newspaper appealing topics for Pensacola Unitarian Universalist Fellowship (PUUF) and ventured in periodically over a couple of years. I was always stimulated by the variety of talks different lay people provided (this preceded professional UU ministry at PUUF) and the lively discussions that followed. I especially loved the vigorous and thoughtful discussions and the spontaneous humor and laughter. But I remained leery of organized religion, and life took me away for a while.

Finally, in 1981 I completed the almighty doctorate, primarily intending to pursue an academic career in magazine journalism. That plan had brought us to Pensacola, where my expected university position fell through with UWF's personnel changes, but Ron was hired at Pensacola Junior College (now Pensacola State College). As Destin started kindergarten, I accepted a spot on the Loyola University of the South Communication Faculty, and our little family endured double lives for two years. Although I loved much about my Loyola and New Orleans experience, ultimately I decided that city, as exciting and appealing as it was in many ways, was not where I wanted to rear our child. So Ron and I chose to make our family and our beloved Pensacola home a priority.

Meanwhile, by age 40, my health, problematic and complex since about age 20, became more unpredictable and time consuming, and contributed to my growing sense that the individual did not, after all, have the control of life that some existentialists assume. Life was increasingly humbling, as life often is.

I enjoyed teaching a wide variety of courses across multiple departments in both local colleges, but the adjunct pay was embarrassing.

By 1987 Ron and I were each thriving as creative independent professionals. We combined forces in Berthelot Consulting Inc., developing original strategies, courses, and seminars, teaching adults in business, industry, organizations, and education, in the Gulf Coast region and around the U.S.

In 1984, we had joined Pensacola Unitarian Universalist Fellowship, which had a minister, but that first minister left suddenly just as I accepted the lay presidency, and the year my Dad died of lymphoma, PUUF became the primary center of our lives, essentially my unpaid full-time job.

My skeptical resistance to any religion had been relieved in late 1984, the day the UUA Principles were finally shared during service. Reassured, I joined that Sunday. Those seven principles fit what I had long believed, and nothing in them violated my sense of authenticity. They are a far cry from the Apostle's Creed, which I had once fervently believed, but could never honestly say again.

The Seven UUA Principles affirm and promote

1. The inherent worth and dignity of every person;
2. Justice, equity and compassion in human relations;
3. Acceptance of one another and encouragement to spiritual growth in our congregations;
4. A free and responsible search for truth and meaning;
5. The right of conscience and the use of the democratic process within our congregations and in society at large;
6. The goal of world community with peace, liberty, and justice for all;
7. Respect for the interdependent web of all existence of which we are a part.

These Principles are not dogma or doctrine, but a guide for those who choose to participate in UU religious communities. They beautifully captured much that I held most dear—and they still do.

The related Sources from Which We Draw suggest a breadth of diversity with which I was/am also comfortable. Those six are adapted in brief below:

1. Direct experience of transcending mystery and wonder, intuition;
2. Words and deeds of prophetic women and men;
3. Wisdom from the world's religions;
4. Jewish and Christian teachings;
5. Humanist teachings and science;
6. Spiritual teachings of earth-centered traditions.

Sources one and five spoke most naturally to me, but I learned constantly from all of them, and loved it.

During my now decades at what became Unitarian Universalist Church of Pensacola, the organization is more structured, the services more similar in style and sometimes substance to more traditional protestant churches; I would prefer a more creative, free-wheeling high discourse hour filled with vigorous conversation and laughter. Many who shared my preferences have dropped out, as others have come. I miss the closer kinship of my past there, but I stay, because there remains much that I value.

Our Principles and our UUCP Covenant, shared in a later chapter, speak deeply to me, and I fully embrace our mission: To celebrate diversity, strive for justice, and inspire love. Those ideals tend to be practiced, not merely preached.

Striving for justice is particularly strong, as among many UU congregations. That's been true for hundreds of years, starting with many notable early Americans, and in Europe before that. Local UUs and members of the Humanists of West Florida are among the most socially active doers in town, especially for their small numbers. Though no longer able to be as active as I'd like, I am happy to support and applaud them.

In the rather conservative Pensacola area, I know of no viable alternative for people like me. Some areas, like Boston, which is the UUA headquarters, many big cities, both coasts, and more liberal Asheville region in the South, have several UU congregations. That abundance can provide more convenience and diversity of options, allowing varying styles and content. All reflect the ideals of our UUA Principles, all draw from the six sources, and all embrace similar covenants and missions. UUCP is the only one within an hour in any direction, and we are grateful to have that.

Early in my time at PUUF, an adult education activity had participants line up on one side of the room if motivated to be there primarily by intellectual needs at one end or primarily by community needs at the other end. I then chose the far intellectual end. My yearning for community had not yet fully formulated in my consciousness, yet it was more vital than I realized and would become ever more so, a primary motivator for much of the rest of my life, even the condo in which I now live.

7

ETHICAL EDUCATION

When our only son was 3 years old, he got passionately into dinosaurs, as often happens. A gifted child, he became rather a prodigy of dinosaurs and related matters. His dino-paleo reading (which was magically early and extensive) led naturally to the topic of evolution. On a family trip to Arkansas, we explored a historic village, and found ourselves in a primitive Baptist Church, pristinely empty except for the three of us and rays of sunlight shining on a chalk board and chalk. Our son automatically walked to the board like a professor and started instructing us about dinosaurs as he drew them, another of his favorite pastimes. In the process, without hesitating, he moved into the topic of evolution, as he then understood it. No doubt it was the only time evolution was preached in that little Baptist church. The walls did not come tumbling down.

By age four or five, Destin had heard the concept of god from somewhere, not us. We had naturally discussed morality and ethics with no mention of god or heaven. One day he made clear that he thought this god idea was the silliest thing he'd ever heard. Uh oh, my darling son was sounding like an absolutist atheist at age 5. I wanted him to feel free to think on his own and freely express himself, yet I was leery of absolutism in kindergarten, and suggested that, in child terms.

"Honey," I said, "that's a big question about which many good and wise people have many different opinions. No one actually knows the right answer. You may not be ready to make that decision permanently at your age."

FEELING FOR AND WITH JESUS

Once when he was even younger, as we browsed in Montgomery Ward, he spotted a crucifix and asked "What happened to that guy?"

I squatted down to look him in the eye as I tried an impromptu explanation of that world-shaking history. Destin was rightfully appalled, as was I. Jesus had been treated abysmally, cruelly, unfairly. We felt for this Jesus, and felt with him. We shared what I believe to be the most vital human trait, *empathy*. Destin did not need god to teach him that important trait or other significant positive human behaviors—which, I believe, grow out of empathy.

In fact, as he grew into middle school, Destin, the non-believer and non-indoctrinated, often behaved far more "Christian like" than some of the other boys in his small up-scale private school. When the group was on an Outward Bound adventure, he automatically insisted on NOT stealing from some stranger's camp. He understood that stealing is wrong, simply wrong. Not because god or Jesus or some other religious leader says so, but because it is not empathetic or compassionate or rational or wise. He wouldn't want it done to him, so why would he do such a thing? It simply made no sense!

This is not meant to suggest that our son was a perfect child or grew into a perfect adult or paragon of virtue now approaching midlife (any more than his parents were or are). He's a good guy, but not a perfect one. Who is? Neither the Christian, Muslim, Buddhist, Jew, Taoist, atheist, agnostic, etc. We are all merely humans, muddling through as best we can. Some try harder than others, and those who make that effort may come from any belief system or none at all.

From about age 6-13, Destin did have the advantage of a very liberal religious education through Unitarian Universalism. That provided some cultural awareness (which is important in America and especially in the Super Christian South), a pluralistic religious and ethnic world view, reinforcement of basic values, and positive interaction with kindred spirits.

But with adults or children, UU promotes no established theological or religious creed that all should believe. Everyone is welcome—Unitarian Christians, Jews, Buddhists, Hindus, Muslims, Humanists, Atheists, all happily congregate in our Sunday services and other events. Of course, people of all races, ethnicities, genders and sexual orientation have long been welcome. Check a UU's religious and personal roots, lifestyles, and perspectives and you might find almost anything, all linked by those UUA Principles and Covenant.

In the middle school period of his private school, Destin experienced a bit of bullying and witnessed some senseless misbehavior and meanness, so when he rather reluctantly went to camp at the UU Camp at the Mountain in Highlands, NC, he returned to express great enthusiasm. "Everybody was so nice," he said. "Why can't everyone act like that?" Indeed.

Again, those UU camp kids were likely behaving for reasons other than god and heaven, which probably weren't preached in their homes or UU churches. Certainly they also weren't perfect, but they were almost certainly no less perfect than the highly controlled highly indoctrinated kids in some private Christian School. Or some Jewish, or Muslim, or other religious institution that might promote "godliness."

8

DYING, DEATH, AND OTHER MYSTERIES

So, what about dying and death, of which all human beings are assured? This awareness of mortality is believed to separate us from other animals, but who knows what other animals know, think, or feel?

For some people, the reality of death is the root and purpose of religious devotion and practice. Years ago a young neighbor, a six- or seven-year-old daughter of a strict fundamentalist Christian family, smiled up at me and said, "I can't wait to die."

I tried not to show my startled response. "Why is that, hon?"

"Oh, 'cause then I get to be with Jesus."

I was so stunned that half a century later, I can clearly see and hear this blond-haired child. If she is still alive, I wonder how she feels now.

I don't recall what I said in return. Probably not much. Likely a stammered "Oh, is that right?"

My own exposure to the moment of dying and death has been limited but soul stirring. Unforgettable. First, the greatest terror of my life was when our seemingly healthy son went into a board-stiff, eyes-rolled-back seizure at 14 months, the exact age that my husband's baby brother had died of an inexplicable seizure.

In an antique shop on T Street, Destin's blue eyes rolled back and he suddenly looked like the still rigor mortis of death. Ron threw him on an antique bed and began what little he knew of CPR, while I got the owner to call an ambulance. Admittedly, I may have prayed then, never mind my beliefs!

Even when it was clear Destin would survive this attack of a rather extreme febrile seizure, there was question of potential brain damage. I have always considered permanently losing one's mind a form of death...

That night I slept in a chair beside Destin's hospital bed as he remained silent and lethargic, not at all himself. An early talker, for months he had chattered constantly.

Around dawn, I was thrillingly startled awake by his happy voice singing one of his favorite ditties, "B-I-N-G-O, B-I-N-G-O, Bingo is his name O!" He stood smiling in the crib. If that seizure was my life's most terrifying moment, this was probably my most grateful. Still, the trauma had been so powerful that I avoided that shop for at least two years, and I could not even ride by it without tearing up.

For three years, Destin stayed on medication with intrusive side effects, had several other febrile seizures, all scary but none comparable to the first. I did anxious round-the-clock checking to make sure he was breathing—until he apparently outgrew the problem. If we had lost him, or lost the him we knew, I can't honestly say what I might have needed to tell myself, what belief system I might have needed to call on. Or denounce.

LOSING MAMA

My humanism served me well with that crisis and with other sadness, losses, and grief, and my more mystical inclination has also played a part. My first experience fully sharing the dying process was with my Mother, who had been fighting colon cancer from age 69 to 70. Although she had excellent home care, we seven siblings shared responsibilities, at least one of us staying with her in our family home all weekends (or more often) during that last year of her life.

As she deteriorated, my Mother once surprised me by speaking admiringly of Dr. Kevorkian as a hero. While I had long believed in the wisdom of self exit with gentle medical assistance, and thus admired this much maligned professional myself, my parents had seemed to be ardent right-to-life advocates who would always oppose "assisted suicide," which I call "compassionate deliverance."

"Mama, you've never said anything like that before!" I exclaimed.

Ever the practical realist, my Mother said simply, "I've never gone through anything like this before."

A KÜBLER-ROSS EXPERIENCE

None of us know how we will react to misery, terror, and death until it comes.

My seemingly pragmatic totally nonreligious older neighbor, a county deputy, had a near death experience with a heart attack. I had read Elizabeth Kübler-Ross by then, heard her speak in person, been impressed and influenced by her studies of people experiencing the death passage, and living to tell about it. Ottry had had no such exposure. Yet what he told me was remarkably similar to those Kübler-Ross reports. In the hospital, while unconscious, he had risen above himself, seen doctors frantically working on him, moved toward a brilliant light, noticed a cherub-like angel perched on a shelf, then come back into his body. He said an attending medical professional later verified much of what he described wit-

41

nessing. This was a remarkable spiritual experience for him, but I don't know that it lured him back to church. Spiritual and religious are not synonymous.

This lawman's wife was an avid member of Unity Church, which tends to be open toward the metaphysical. Although I had had no meaningful woo woo experiences since the "Brian" warnings decades before, I accompanied Melanee to a visiting psychic or intuitive at Unity. We were sitting in the back quarter of a packed room, both raising our hands to be considered, along with many others. The speaker called on me. I said nothing. He described my home, a story and a half 1928 bungalow raised on brick pillars, a quirky porch-wrapped cottage that I loved, and not at all standard fare. Mine was the only home he mentioned. He included details like old, wood and brick, raised up off ground, and 14 steps. Then he suddenly said with alarm, "Smoke! I smell smoke, in the kitchen!" The day before, for the first and only time, I had come into the kitchen to discover newspapers sitting too near an electric oven, smoldering, about to burst into flames. I had narrowly averted disaster—which this stranger saw and smelled.

Once again, my awareness of and appreciation for the metaphysical, mental communication, and other mysteries was piqued, affirming Hamlet's famous quote "...There are more things in heaven and earth, Horatio, than are dreamt of in your philosophy."

Perhaps it was around this period that I read physicist Arthur Koestler's *Roots of Coincidence: An Excursion into Parapsychology*, which further tweaked my imagination and opened that window to possibility.

Some other library user had filled that book with notes and comments. Although I'd never write in library books, I related to that stranger's questions and remarks and felt a tremendous connection.

I happened to be with my Mother on what became the last weekend of her life, along with a Hospice nurse who attended for the first time. About 4 am, September 13, 1993, Mom went into a coma. The nurse woke me and said it was time to summon my siblings, scattered in Dallas, Pensacola, and Baton Rouge, as well as Bogalusa. One by one they arrived to say their goodbyes. Mama began losing breath, having longer and longer periods between breaths, each time making us expect it would be her last. Our baby brother Malcolm, her only son, was the last to arrive. We feared "Mal" wouldn't make it in time. As he rushed in and told Mom how much he loved her, she breathed for the last time, and was at peace.

After remaining controlled enough to be writing her obituary while waiting for her passage, I then shocked myself and everyone there by collapsing in unfettered anguish.

TWO SWALLOWTAILS

Minutes later, I composed myself. Mama's closest local first cousins happened to arrive at the side family door, not knowing she had just died. I greeted them, told them of her passing, and was drawn, lured, pulled outside by the largest, loveliest butterfly I had ever seen. It hovered over one of Mother's favorite bushes (she had taken up gardening in later life). I walked out as if in a trance, knelt in the grass beside that bush. My face practically touched the butterfly. That exquisite creature made no effort to flee. We had what

I could only describe as a mystical communication. I had not yet known that butterflies are pan culturally associated with life's biggest transition. This beauty seemed like what I now know as a swallowtail, perhaps yellow and black, though I most remember black and red, colors I particularly associate with my Mother. Being 100% Lebanese, Mama had nearly black hair and eyes and looked great in red and black. Several family members witnessed this awe-inspiring moment, and all soon learned to associate such butterflies with our Mother.

Fast forward 19 years to September 2012, the scattering of my husband Ron's ashes, in a simple post-Sunday service ceremony, outside our Pensacola Unitarian Universalist Church. Our beloved minister emeritus had just returned from traveling in time to lead this small event. Rev. Bob Eddy was saying some free-flowing personal words about Ron when I noticed a bustling flurry among my attending sisters and their teen and young adult children. When I turned to see what was happening, I too saw the butterfly, so like the one that had appeared moments after my Mother's death. She felt with us. I had to share the story with all present. Some family members that had reacted, had learned only through family lore. They were unborn, too young or not around to witness the original experience.

Such moments make impressions. Nine years after the swallowtail at the scattering of Ron's ashes, a UUCP friend in a small group Halloween Zoom discussion brought up this butterfly story. I hadn't even recalled she attended Ron's event, yet she happened to mention this experience. There is value in remembering and in sharing our personal stories, our special moments and cherished memories. Share yours while you can; and don't omit the mysteries.

RON'S DECLINE AND END

While mystical moments are meaningful, humanism was far more relevant in dealing with the long, confusing, frustrating, painful, period of my husband's physical and mental decline, dementia, likely Parkinson's, bleeding stroke, total disability, and choice to die. I have explored this ordeal and my early widowhood in a longer soon-to-be-published book, **IMPERFECT LOVE**, *a reluctant caretaker's memoir of passages and choices*, but it must be touched on here.

As I grappled with how to handle Ron and even whether to care for him myself, I was fortified both by organizational input, such as that from Alzheimer's Family Services and later Hospice, and by generous repeat assistance by a select few friends and family. It was surprising and heartwarming who came through. And surprising and disappointing who didn't.

Come to think of it, almost all the best direct help with my sick and dying husband and after his passing came from non-religious friends and family that I would consider humanists—whether they use the term or not. While their varying roots included Catholic, Jewish, and Protestant, none were then active in a traditional faith. They were simply good, kind, loving people I could count on. While many others contributed in ways I fully appreciate, I honestly don't know what we would have done without that small core of stalwart supporters, along with the occasional visits, calls, cards, foods, and other gentle gifts of many.

Words helped as well. Though I happen to be a non-alcoholic teetotaler, I often reflected on (my slight adaptation of) the powerful little AA prayer: "May I have the serenity to accept the things I cannot change, the courage to change the things I can, and the wisdom to know the difference." Isn't that wisdom the toughest challenge?

Also, this UUCP Covenant became a sort of mantra that gave me solace and strength. It is similar to that of many UU communities: "Love is the spirit of this Church, and service its law. This is our covenant—to dwell together in peace, seek the truth in love, and help one another." It became my "covenant" with Ron.

CHOICES, CHOICES, CHOICES

Rev. Bob Eddy had long before influenced our perspective on the right to die with dignity, so it was natural for Ron to choose his final exit after years of worsening dementia and nearly a year of intensified loss from his destructive stroke. While he couldn't get himself a glass of water or sometimes find his way to the toilet, he still knew everyone important and mentally remained competent to make that choice.

Still, when he suddenly, silently, and emphatically halted all eating and drinking without explanation, it was excruciating. Almost every one of my closest friends and family happened to be across the country at that crucial time. Both our ministers were also. Timing could not have been worse.

Our son hastily flew in from Los Angeles and (with a Hospice nurse and a hospital bed in our living room) we faced what became an arduous yet cherished 10-day death watch. Sharing the dying process with a loved one is painful, powerful, precious, and profound.

Again, some personal choice is evident, even with the patient in an end-stage coma. When our friend Ida stopped in on her way back into town and whispered her message in Ron's ear, I went to the bathroom and Destin happened to walk outside. Ida left. The nurse suddenly yelled for me to come back. Ron's breathing became intermittent, as my Mom's had. I asked the nurse to run get Destin while I quickly said my last words to my husband of 45 years. "Please breathe and wait just a moment for Destin to run back in," I pleaded. And he did. As our son and I held Ron's hands, he left this world.

As far as we know, he will live again only in our hearts, so that must be enough. Should death prove us wrong, it will be a wonder-full surprise.

Three days later, the Celebration of Ron's life was unique to him and to us. Not a word about god or heaven or afterlife, but much about this good man and our lives together. A fabulous musical trio of friends welcomed a packed crowd in with Fat's Domino's "Walkin' to New Orleans" and sent all out with a rousing "When the Saints Go Marching In." In between were other jazzy mid-century New Orleans style rhythm and blues, a stunning aria of "Ave Maria" (a nod to our Catholic roots and Catholic families), and many personal stories, including some conflicting memories by raucous "dueling Cajuns," Ron's two brothers who had us both crying and laughing uproariously.

At the reception, one person raving about the experience was a prominent, rather staid older Jewish businessman who surprised me saying, "I usually hate funerals, Dolly, but this was the best one I've ever been to!" He wistfully added, "I wish I could have something like that when I go."

47

"Well, why can't you?" I asked. But he only shrugged rather hopelessly.

Why do so many people assume they must live and die according to the norms and assumptions of others? Although I have learned we can't always have our preferred choices about everything, as the young existentialist me had wished, we can often choose more freely than we tend to do. How we exit and how we send off those we love should certainly be among those free choices.

10

VISION: INFINITE EVOLUTION?

Following my young adult certitude of existential nothing-ness after death, another theory intuitively came to me in the mid-1990s, and still makes sense. It's suggested by the earlier flea-dog remark and is mostly nothing I've read in any book, or it preceded my reading anything similar, though some related thinking showed up later during my years participating in a local Theosophy group and reading some Buddhist, Taoist, and other Eastern writers. Somehow, my own sense of ongoing post-death human evolution (suggested below in poems of that time) came to me during and right after attending the classic play "Our Town." I don't know what concrete aspect of that drama so illuminated this sudden and instinctive spiritual awareness, but it was a quantum leap beyond my previous thinking. What if, I wondered, the evolution we understand is barely the beginning? What if humans are not the end of evolution but merely a step along the way—and evolution goes way way beyond us? Maybe psychics, intuitives, saints, auras, and even angels that some experience are glimmers of next steps, minor breakthroughs of the ever higher and yet higher realm, onto, perhaps, infinity?

Once these thoughts occurred to me, they naturally evolved into poetry. These several were all written around that time, each with a bit of light humor:

IGNORANT BUGS

1996

My body is full
of organisms
that know me not a bit
but feed in blissful ignorance
when I am less than fit.

Though I'm a source
of their existence
I'm well beyond their ken
Never mind our symbiosis,
they'll never comprehend!

Still no less a vital part
of what they can not understand
bacteria and viruses
are integral to man.

And may offer a model
for evolution that goes on
if in the cosmic scheme of things
we are a measly prawn.
Our human minds then
not the end
but a means
to the beyond
beyond our meager limits
beyond the gods we grasp

beyond our puny visions
stuck in our muddy pasts.

Perhaps humans also can evolve
transmute, transcend, and grow
into more than we imagine
into more than we can know
if like the critters in ourselves
we've more potential than we show.

I'll cling to that
for entertainment
and some ethereal hope
but it surely makes no difference
How I live, behave, or cope.

For any gods beyond our ken
will embrace the dumb as well
and if they are worth-knowing gods
will send no one to hell—
except perhaps the know-it-alls
so sure, so small, so smug
swimming in false certitude
with no more cosmic insight
than our last intestinal bug.

WHAT A GAS!
1996

"What is God?" the nuns asked.
"God is the Supreme Being who made all
things," we droned.

Tidy bit of nothing, that
simply saying god is god.

For decades since
I have assumed
that god is simply not.

Now I suspect
that god may be a gas:
transforming the firmament
lighting our world
erupting Vesuvius
drifting around dangerously
or merely slipping
indiscreetly
out human butts.

I suspect that god
may be a gas,
Pele personified, multiplied, intensified,
creator and destroyer
visible and invisible
oddly essential to all life.

Awesome, powerful,
truly humbling force
only as omniscient
and omnipresent
as the very air we breathe.
Only the mysterious difference
between life and death.

SLINKY

1996

What if existence
were a spiral,
infinite spiral
curved into itself—
end kissing beginning
and vice versa
future past present
birth growth death
back again forward
retreats, renewals,
endless epiphanies
seamless circles
of cosmic spirals,
all one Super Slinky
stretching
bouncing
twisting
toy
of playful gods.

What if existence ...

11

TRULY AWESOME!

That word "awesome" is about as overused these days as others that annoy me (particularly recent bombardments ending with "right?" And beginning with "So...")—but I'd like to briefly address awe, true awe. To be awed is the essence of mysticism, as I perceive it. When I call myself a mystical humanist. I certainly do not mean acetic or other self denial features commonly associated with mystics. I'm actually a pretty gluttonous mystic!

If the humanist aspect is seen as the totally rational, logical, reasonable application of human behavior that sustains human life, for me, the mystical is the awesome aspect—stunning moments that enrich life, make life especially worth living. It is the ineffable stuff of poetry and art and music and dance, of being profoundly awed by beauty, by nature, by natural miracles too often ignored, by coincidences, and unexplained phenomena, and by life itself. Beyond awe, no, within awe, is gratitude. In spite of problems, I find myself immensely grateful to be here, savoring the good and the beautiful.

My personal obsession of recent years is the sky we share, notably clouds and light, and the water below them. That obsession started before I moved into my 4th floor bayside condo, and has been nourished by this location, stimulating endless photos snapped from my balcony, and poems and even a story book of playful Cloud Cherubs (for which I seek the right illustrator in order to publish soon). However this world got here, I feel a responsibility to appreciate it, to savor it, and consciously feel and express thanks to and for all.

Thanks to whom? Some might wonder. Doesn't matter. Maybe to the cosmos. What matters is the feeling. Appreciation and gratitude are inherently positive. They are their own reward.

SIMPLE SKIES

2016

Moon sneaks over shutters,
Gleaming eye half shut
And peeks into my bedroom.
I welcome the intruder
With a smile.

Yesterday,
I paused my rush
To pool exercise
To admire pillowing bundles
Of white fluff'
Resting on blue sheets
Behind the school's red brick clock tower

Later, slowing through a deluge
Along Bayfront Parkway,
I'm captivated:
The sudden summer storm
Rewards me with
Roiling charcoal clouds,
Dramatic artwork over pearl waters.

When did skies
Start to mean so much to me?

After decades shrouded
By sprawling mossy oak trees,
And sheltered by deep eaves,
I now crave skies,
All aspects, all seasons.

Frankly, I had, before,
mostly ignored the heavens.
They were merely there, like air.

Oh, I have always needed beauty,
And certainly I savored sunsets,
Especially sunsets over seas,

But, lately I relish,
more than ever before,
The skies themselves,
Whatever their state,
Whatever lies below.

Why this deepened appreciation?
Did Age re-awaken my awareness
With new gratitude
For the always precious
Ever-changing view above?

PTERODACTYL CLOUD

2018

Gargantuan
Pterodactyl Cloud
Emerges from behind the high rise
Dwarfing all else.
Beaked face,
White against blue sky
Giant wings outstretched
Bruised gray underbelly,
Stormy, gurgling.

Not really a dinosaur,
Experts say,
But I first met it as such,
When my then young son
Fed his dino passion.

Pterodactyl
Perhaps is bird-related,
A curator later explained,
And I was hooked.

I live in the cracks,
The borders,
The not fully understood,
The thin, fluid line
Between this and that,
Overlapping realities,
Mysteries.

I like it here.
Head in the clouds?
Perhaps.

The vaporous pterosaur moves forward,
Past drifting into present,
As Past is wont to do.

Within moments,
He dissipates,
Extinct again.
For now.

Suddenly, a Blue Angels jet
Roars into view
Piercing the void.
Transmutation?

SPLENDIFEROUS!

2021

Driving down Scenic Highway
I gasp and almost swerve
Toward Escambia Bay,
Toward the widest, wildest,
Most exquisite rainbow
I have ever seen.
Splendiferous!

I tend to avoid 4 syllable words
When simpler will suffice
and I have long wondered
What could warrant

Such hifalutin praise.
The Grand Canyon, of course,
And Sistine Chapel.
Each once moved me to tears.
But their glories were expected,
I had traveled far to see them.
They deserved, but did not demand,
That descriptor. This does.
Now, I'm merely heading home
From a pleasant family lunch.

So, splendiferous!
Splendamndiferous!!

Broad watercolor bands of brilliant hues
Arch over the bright white bridge
As if engineered by a creative god
To hold up that passageway.

Turbulent dark and darker clouds
Fight against the sun streams
But can't hold back the breakthrough beams
....At least for a moment.

As I speed toward space to pull over
For a better view
And photos, of course,
It all changes, reconfigures
Into an ordinary dreary gray day.

But for one stunning moment,
I have glimpsed Nature's Miracle,

And that is enough.

12

CRISES AND COMMON GOOD

Not all surprises are pleasant. But we can learn and grow from each one. We are now grappling with a world more complex, turbulent, and problematic than most of us ever expected to face. A pandemic has put some other issues into sharper focus, and how we handle that pandemic illustrates how we may navigate the other challenges now upon us—and those yet to come.

SAVING OURSELVES

2020

I like Liberty, really I do.
Justice too.

And privacy matters to me
To a prudent degree.
These very American virtues
We want to maintain.
They're worth some struggle,
Worth some strain.
Even worth a little pain.

But a pandemic makes some NEW demands.
The Future rests in all our hands.
And in our mouths and noses, you see,
Where vile germs can flow,

From you and from me.
Illness, debilitation, and death,
Erupting, attacking from our poisonous breath.

We each have great power
To shield ourselves and others too.
You can save me, and I can save you.
So let's save each other,
Me, you; you, me.
A little discomfort
Can change destiny.

...But only if we all give a damn
And are willing to do
All that we can.
Really, so little is required,
Vax, masks and distancing,
Till COVID's expired.

Liberty, justice, privacy,
Not so simple these days.
Your "freedom" could mean everyone pays.
Your "liberty" may snatch mine away
And if your "privacy" hides the monsters you spread,
Innocent bystanders may soon be dead.
How is that justice? How is that fair?
Reality proves we must now beware
Of risky behaviors we perilously share
Simply by commingling "bugs" in our air.

If only we could SEE these foul beasts
Devouring people for their feasts
I have no doubt sane folks
Would back up with ease
And likely shout out
In shock, fear, and pleas,
To strangers and kin—
And view nonchalance
As a serious sin!

Unfortunately, this invisible foe
When ignored will continue
To grow and to grow.

What's most demanded
If we are to win,
Is a deep, deep commitment
Now to begin:
Beyond other virtues
I wish we all would
Profoundly commit
To Our Common Good!

Without that practice
From people at large,
Let's face it, this virus
Is the Master in Charge...

LET'S TRY *INTER*DEPENDENCE

When young, I hungered for independence. I was eager to be independent from my parents, not because they were bad parents, but because, well, they were my parents. Once mentally emancipated, I considered marriage only with a man who shared my desire for mutual respect and professional independence, rather than typical patterns of the 1960s, certainly the 1960s South. In fact, Ron and I were both eager to leave the small-mindedness of our respective Louisiana hometowns and explore the world. We wanted independence from our very roots, some aspects of which we found shameful. Of course, the more I saw of the world, the more I realized that human problems are not geographically limited!

Like many who have loved and lost, now I would give anything to have my parents again. When my Dad had his first massive coronary at age 49, I raced back from Turkey, quite willingly, for his open-heart surgery, forfeiting the rambling life I loved. I could have done nothing less. Families are naturally interdependent. While my marriage had that essential independence and mutual respect for each other as individuals, it also developed vital interdependence. A long relationship, even an imperfect one, naturally becomes interdependent.

I've also come to recognize deep connection to my roots, from which no one can be totally independent. While I have railed against racism since the 1960's—as a college student, daily newspaper editor and Black Studies teacher in the late '60s/early '70s and a "unity in diversity" consultant and trainer in the '80s and '90s and beyond, I now cherish other aspects of my own heritage (Lebanese, German, and even Bogalusa, Louisiana, Southern). Yet I notice and acknowledge my white privilege and subtle residues of racism in my own thoughts and behavior—without denial, resistance, rancor, or unproductive guilt.

WE ALL NEED ONE ANOTHER

I now understand that we ALL truly depend on one another, we all need one another. The whole of society benefits from the best of its parts, and that best may come from unexpected sources.

My upgraded, colorized, and republished little book, *PERFECTLY SQUARE, A Fantasy Fable for All Ages*, uses a lighthearted allegory of geometric shapes to inspire us to embrace and use everyone's gifts. Both the 1994 and current version of *PERFECTLY SQUARE* is "Dedicated to all who value the variety of our ever-changing world and appreciate the interdependence that makes us one."

Never has our need for interdependent awareness, attitude, and behavior been more important, more urgent, than now. COVID-19 has shown that need. The elderly, those in nursing homes, medical workers, people of color, the obese, the poor, the homeless, immigrants, the undocumented, prisoners, anyone in packed housing, detention centers, and workplaces, anyone with underlying medical conditions— these are the most vulnerable, the most likely to die—and to spread COVID. So, do they matter? If we didn't know, as we now do, that people of all ages and circumstances may also get desperately ill and die—and perhaps contaminate us—would our humanity make us care about the most vulnerable, make us strive to protect them as well as everyone else?

We are so fortunate to now have vaccines to help us protect ourselves and others. Vaccines, boosters, sanitation, continuing masks and distancing as needed, these are our collective weapons against this dangerous foe. Do we care enough about ourselves and others to use them for the greater good? Certainly my logical humanism and Unitarian Universalism demand it. But I would think, so does every religion on earth. Remember that little Golden Rule?

We are all inter-connected simply by being human. As a child I looked at the night sky and predicted, "If Earth is ever invaded by aliens from other planets, we would probably all unite—old differences wouldn't matter."

COVID-19 is our invading alien. We can't see it, we don't know who has it, we don't know to whom we may give it. And we don't know if our cavalier behavior may bring mild or serious illness, or life ruin, or death.

We DO now know what needs to be done: Vaccinate all who can be vaccinated. Follow CDC guidelines for masking, distancing, hand washing, and sanitizing as needed, quarantine and isolate as circumstances require. Do you practice that? Do most people in your sphere? If not, why not? Even when lives depend on our behavior, do we not recognize and accept the obvious interdependence on which we all must rely?

Much sooner than expected, vaccines became available. Safe, well-tested vaccines. That should have been the end of COVID-19, or mostly so. We had a real weapon. Multitudes took it with gratitude, and little ill effect. Others, often the same ones who refused masks and other safeguards, simply said No! Nope, and you can't make me, like an obstinate 2-year-old.

In the 1970's in Europe, I was fortunate to hear cultural anthropologist Margaret Mead speak. One line stays with me. "There are no fences in the sky." Her focus then was pollution and atomic bombs. While those certainly remain pertinent, the concept also holds true for viral pandemics. There are no fences in the air we share, yet we must be careful to create safeguards, boundaries—to protect, not only ourselves, but every other person with whom we come into contact—or the harm can multiply exponentially.

The US and the world have already suffered horribly, and largely unnecessarily, from the virulent Delta variant. Now a new Omicron variant threatens. Who knows what Omicron may do, or what's next? How we respond is crucial!

Some people grouse that following CDC guidelines and getting vaccinated infringes on their liberty. I say ventilators are not very liberating! Some shrug, "I leave it to God." I ask, "Did your God not give us brains with which to think and feel and care about others?" If Jesus understood a mask and vaccines could protect others, wouldn't Jesus wear a mask and take the vaccine? It is literally a shot at life for many—and increased protection for all with whom they come into contact. The more who are protected, the less likely we are to have more powerful and destructive viruses evolve.

UNEXPECTED ADVANTAGES?

Along with its horrors, this pandemic may also have some positive effects, both for individuals and for society. Some dear friends and family members have used the cloistered circumstances to grow personally and artistically. While many businesses suffered terribly, others tried something new and benefited. For awhile, the air cleared. In parts of the world, it cleared spectacularly, at least temporarily. Have you found unexpected advantages along with the miseries?

The pandemic may have contributed to the incredible righteous uprisings in response to the flagrant George Floyd murder and too many other examples of police brutality and justice injustices. Black Lives Matter demonstrations include people of all ethnicities and backgrounds, as never before. Our long and challenging cloister may have spurred some participation. But I hope that, at some deep level, this coronavirus pandemic has helped multitudes here and around the globe become more aware of our interdependence, more inclined to act for Our Common Good.

If the protesters, the police, and others are vaccinated, remain peaceful, wear masks, and try to distance, we may actually survive and benefit from a better world. A safer, healthier world; a fairer, more equitable, more compassionate world; a world that recognizes, preserves, and nurtures the best of everyone, rather than assuming the worst.

Climate change is an ongoing challenge demanding our collective cooperation. Climate change proves its own reality through the current barrage of various storms, floods, fires, and other horrific upheavals and more subtle results, such as the dwindling monarchs and disappearances of whole species. Check the patterns of the last decade and imagine what comes next.

WHERE ARE WE HEADED?

This Chinese maxim is worth pondering: "If you continue in the direction you are headed, you will surely get where you are going." Where are we headed—as individuals, as communities, as a nation, as a world? Is it where we want to go?

We don't have to believe together to work together for the greater good. We can differ in background, heritage, socio-economics, gender, sexuality, age, politics, religion, etc. and STILL care about one another as human beings. Still strive to contribute to, not detract from the Common Good. That is the overriding mandate for humanity to survive and thrive. It is suggested by the Golden Rule and by every religion and belief system known on earth. It is the essence of Humanism and suggested and implied by the oneness of Mysticism. It is also simply logical. We ARE in this together...

COVID-19 is presumably temporary. But our response to it suggests how we may respond to the next calamity. Or the one after that. A year or a century from now, in our personal lives and in society at large, there will be new crises, new traumas, new challenges. And new opportunities. What matters is how we deal with each one. Will we operate from a perspective of interdependence? Of recognizing our oneness and caring for our shared humanity? Will we tend to cooperate for Our Common Good? Or will we continue to be mired in strife and antipathy so toxic that it poisons us all? Will we flourish or perish?

True, freedom and independence are beautiful, essential. They go hand and hand with individualism, all proudly representing the USA. But with those alone active, we may not survive. And certainly will not thrive. Let's also promote, foster, and celebrate an essential—and I hope growing—spirit of Interdependence. Mutual devotion to Our Common Good demands this understanding and appreciation of interdependence. Our relationships, our communities, our country, and our earth will be better for that move forward in a positive direction. Together.Together!

PERTINENT WEBSITES

Unitarian Universalist Church of Pensacola
    (https://uupensacola.org)
Unitarian Universalist Association
    (https://uua.org)
Humanists of West Florida
    (https://humanistsofwestflorida.org)
American Humanist Association
    (https://americanhumanist.org)
The Theosophical Society
    (https://theosophicalsociety.org)
Unity (https://unity.org)
American Ethical Union (https://aeu.org)

About Dr. Dolly Haik-Adams Berthelot

Each part of **Dr. Dolly Berthelot's** meandering professional and personal life has enriched one another and led to where she is today: an intellectually thriving though physically unpredictable 77-year-old author with countless articles and poems and several quite varying books published across decades—and more now waiting in line. Her career has included innovative public school and university teaching, communication consulting and original seminars with Unity in Diversity emphasis; daily newspaper writer and editor; international magazine travel writing and photography; and art photography.

Now a widow after 45 years of marriage, "Dr Dolly" adjusted well to the pandemic and enjoys her "mostly writing" life in a warm and friendly high rise condo overlooking beautiful Pensacola Bay. She also works there individually assisting limited select clients with writing, editing, and interpersonal communication. Life story writing and memoirs became her forte, as addressed in mineyourmemories1.com.

She conceived the concept "Scars to Stars" in this book and then recommended it as the standard title for the exciting new Energion series kicked off by *SCARS TO STARS*. She will serve as series consulting editor.

Her only son lives in Los Angeles.

About This Series

"What makes night within us may leave stars"
— Victor Hugo, *Ninety Three.*

Mini-Memoirs—Scars to Stars. This new Energion Publications series of short books provides provocative brief memoirs portraying diverse spiritual, religious, or ethical journeys by select authors.

Experience shapes beliefs, and in turn, behaviors, often more than we realize. Ideally we learn and grow from the various paths that determine our destinations. Painful moments can lead to unexpected joy. Insight and inspiration also come from the cogently shared memories and perspectives of others, both those similar to and different from ourselves.

Mini-Memoirs—Scars to Stars derives its title, and indeed its mission from those words used in the first volume of the series, *SCARS TO STARS* by Dr. Dolly Haik-Adams Berthelot, who is also series consulting editor.

May these books stimulate your own memories, nourish your own creativity, and help guide your own journey.

Endorsements

I love this book. Dolly Berthelot writes beautifully whether she's telling stories from her wide ranging life or articulating observations on religion and the human condition. Readers will be captivated by adventures from her Catholic roots in small town Louisiana, a doomed but transformative young love, innovative and controversial teaching and publications advising, international living, and finally starting her own consulting firm. SCARS TO STARS is smart and entertaining—fun, but also a profound read!

Deirdre Barrett
Lecturer at Harvard Medical School,
and author of *Pandemic Dreams*
and *The Committee of Sleep.*

I thoroughly enjoyed this story of youthful discovery to senior acknowledgement of the mystery of human existence. It reminded me of my spiritful youth and adult journey of finding the awe in our universe and putting my faith in humanity. I believe it will do the same for readers in their quest for the stars in their lives, and who also bear the scars of life as well, all so warmly versed in her story, poetry, and prose.

Celebrant Andre (Buz) Ryland
Founder, Humanists of West Florida

I read SCARS TO STARS before sunrise on my 69th birthday. It seemed appropriate to listen to another seeker's story as I pondered the meaning of my life. This book celebrates the moral arc of history that consciously and unconsciously guides our spiritual journeys, affirming that ethics, wonder, and Mysticism are not restricted to any religious tradition or belief system. Dolly Berthelot invites us to listen to our own lives, to hear the deeper movements of wisdom, as she shares her own story. I am grateful to have encountered this book and recommend it for seekers, questioners, and persons certain of their faith, as a reminder that wherever we are there are lessons to be learned, for we are on holy ground.

Bruce Epperly, PhD
Professor, University Administrator, and Chaplain

Dolly Berthelot's little book is a big challenge to those who dismiss non-Christians as unlikely providers of value to our world; her life refutes that canard and connects humanism to the highest values of the human experience.

Rev. Steve Kindle
Social Justice Activist, Author, and Pastor

www.ingramcontent.com/pod-product-compliance
Lightning Source LLC
Chambersburg PA
CBHW031608040426
42452CB00006B/446